THE GREAT CASTLE SEARCH

Jane Bingham

Illustrated by Dominic Groebner

Designed by Stephen Wright

Edited by Jane Chisholm
Castles consultant: Dr. Abigail Wheatley

Contents

About this book

This is a book about castles and the people who lived in them. But it's also a challenging puzzle book. You can see below how the puzzles work.

The aim of each puzzle is to spot all the people, animals and objects in the scenes. If you are stuck, you can turn to pages 28 to 31 for help.

The strip at the top of the page tells you where and when the castle in the picture was built.

Around the edge of the big scene are lots of little pictures.

The writing next to each little picture tells you how many of that thing you can find in the big scene.

Some little pictures are shown from a different angle than the ones in the big scene.

Some of the things you are searching for may be partly hidden, but they still count.

The story of castles

A thousand years ago, the world was a very dangerous place. Kings and lords needed somewhere safe to shelter while they fought off attacks. So they started building castles.

The castle provided a home for the lord and his family, his servants and his soldiers. It was also a place of safety for all the people who lived on the lord's land. Whenever an enemy attacked, everyone ran for cover to the castle.

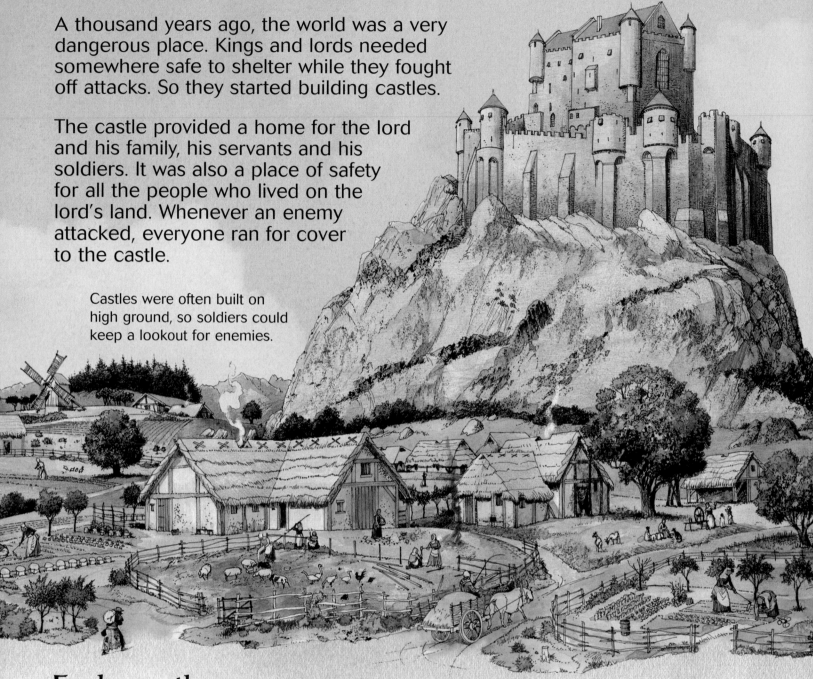

Castles were often built on high ground, so soldiers could keep a lookout for enemies.

Early castles

The first castles were built around the year 900. At first, they were simply strong homes surrounded by banks of earth. But by around 1050 some people were building more complicated structures.

In England and France, kings and lords built 'motte and bailey' castles. These early castles had a tall tower which stood on a mound (or motte), and a walled area known as a bailey. Most people lived in the bailey, but when an enemy attacked everyone sheltered in the tower.

Some early castles had wooden towers, but people soon started building with stone because it was much stronger.

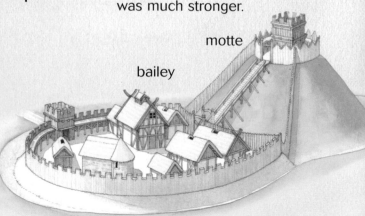

motte

bailey

Changing shapes

By the 1300s, armies had developed a terrifying range of weapons. So builders found new ways to make their castles stronger. They built extra walls, with walkways, watchtowers and gatehouses.

Around 1400, soldiers started blasting castle walls with cannons. People no longer felt safe in castles, and the castle as a place of refuge was on its way out.

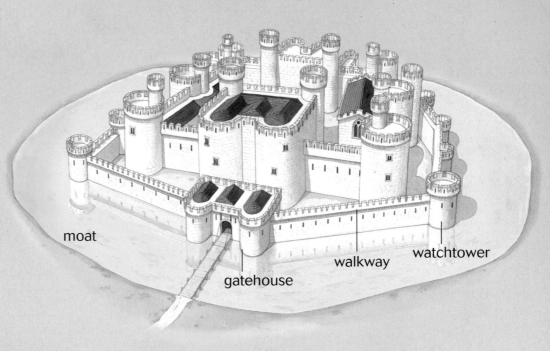

moat

gatehouse

walkway

watchtower

Heavily defended castles like this were first built by crusader knights fighting in the Middle East.

This romantic castle was built in Germany in the 1860s.

The end of the castle?

By the 1500s, most people had stopped building castles. But many rulers still wanted strong, protected homes. Samurai lords in Japan lived in tall fortresses, while Mogul emperors in India built massive forts from marble and stone.

In the 1800s, some people began to take an interest in castles again. Since then, a few wealthy individuals have built themselves 'mock' castles to live in. These romantic buildings look like medieval castles, but they were never intended for war.

An early castle

After the Normans conquered England in 1066, they forced the Saxon people to build castles.

Many castles had a tower on a mound, or 'motte', and a walled 'bailey', where the soldiers lived.

Norman soldiers were in charge. Find 17 Normans giving orders and watching the Saxons at work.

Carpenters sawed up wood. Spot six carpenters sawing wood.

The castle was protected by a palisade of wooden stakes. Find six workers building the palisade.

A winch was used to lift heavy loads. Can you see the winch?

Castle building could be very dangerous. Spot the falling Saxon.

Sometimes workers took a break. Spot 14 workers having their lunch break.

The castle was surrounded by a ditch. Find 19 Saxons with shovels working on the ditch.

Sometimes workers dropped their tools. Spot two dropped hammers.

Building materials were carried on stretchers and sleds. Find 12 stretchers and three sleds.

Some buildings had thatched roofs made from straw. Spot 17 workers laying or transporting straw.

The castle had three drawbridges. Can you find them?

Lookouts watched out for enemies. Find nine lookouts on the tower and the palisade.

Some people still worked on farms while the castle was built. Spot three farm workers.

Parts of the castle were covered in limewash. Find six builders applying limewash.

In the great tower

Many castles had a great tower, built from stone. The tower was the strongest part of the castle,

and also the grandest. This was where the lord sometimes stayed and entertained his guests.

Merchants came to visit the lord. Find three merchants.

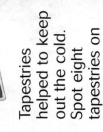

Tapestries helped to keep out the cold. Spot eight tapestries on the walls.

The tower had steep spiral staircases. Spot the servant falling down the steps.

Religious services were held in the chapel. Can you see three priests?

Looking out for enemies was hungry work. Find the guards having a snack.

Prisoners were captured and held in a bare room. Can you find seven prisoners?

8

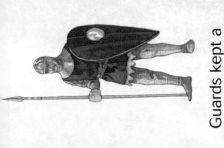

Guards kept a look out for signs of trouble. Find 28 guards on and off duty.

Wooden buckets were used to hold water. Spot 19 buckets of water.

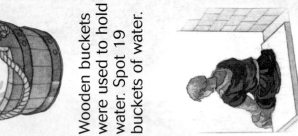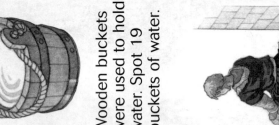

The castle toilet was called the garderobe. Spot a guard on the garderobe.

There was enough food stored to last for months. Find 27 sacks of flour and 28 barrels of wine.

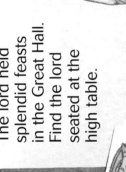

The lord held splendid feasts in the Great Hall. Find the lord seated at the high table.

The steward was in charge of the castle accounts. Spot the steward counting his money.

The lord's family stayed in a room called the solar. Find the lady working on her tapestry.

A clerk checked that none of the stores were missing. Can you see the clerk?

In the bailey

The walled area around the great tower was known as the bailey. It was full of people working hard to keep the castle running well. Most of the cooking for the castle was done in the bailey.

Carpenters made furniture and carts. Find a carpenter making a wheel.

Laundry maids spread their washing on bushes. Spot eight tunics drying on the bushes.

Cooks used large cauldrons. Can you see six cauldrons?

Carters arrived with food. Spot 10 turnips that have fallen out of this cart.

Milkmaids carried milk from the castle dairy. Find three milkmaids.

Bakers had large outdoor ovens. Find 16 loaves of bread.

Hunters brought home animals to cook. Spot two deer and eight rabbits.

Blacksmiths made and mended tools and weapons. Find 12 swords being made in the blacksmiths' forge.

Some servants had the job of sharpening knives. Can you see the three knife grinders?

The stables could get quite smelly. Spot five stable boys mucking out the stables.

Farriers made shoes for horses. Find the farrier shoeing a horse.

Children played a kind of football. Spot seven children playing with a ball.

Fletchers made wooden shafts for arrows. Find 13 arrows.

Geese were fattened up for feasts. Spot seven geese.

Under siege

During the Middle Ages, castles were often attacked by enemies, and a siege could last for months.

The attackers had some terrifying weapons, but the soldiers under siege fought back fiercely.

Trumpeters gave musical orders to the soldiers. Spot three trumpeters.

Rocks were fired from giant catapults. Find 30 rocks waiting to be fired.

Some soldiers tried to swim across the moat. Spot four swimming men.

Siege towers were wheeled close to the walls. Find 11 men in a siege tower.

Many archers used longbows. Spot 13 longbows.

Some wounded soldiers fell from the battlements. Find three falling defenders.

Dead animals were catapulted into the castle to spread disease. Spot the flying cow.

Knights had shields showing their family's coat of arms. Find 53 shields.

Some archers fired bolts from crossbows. Find six crossbows.

Sometimes an enemy spy sneaked into the castle in disguise. Spot the spy.

Mounted knights fought with violent weapons. Find this morning star.

Defenders dropped pots of flaming liquid. Spot four pots of fire.

Archers fired through slits in castle walls called arrow loops. Find 20 arrow loops.

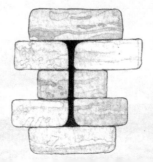

Daring soldiers climbed scaling ladders. Spot six climbing or falling attackers.

At a feast

Sometimes the lord of the castle held a lavish feast in the Great Hall. Important guests sat at the high table, and merchants and knights joined in too. Feasts were very noisy and lasted for hours.

The castle cats and dogs gobbled up the scraps. Spot four cats and four dogs.

Jugglers entertained the guests. Find 11 juggling balls.

The castle servants worked very hard. Can you see six?

Cooks made elaborate dishes from marzipan. Look for the marzipan castle.

The salt container was shaped like a ship. Can you spot it?

Guests drank from gold and silver goblets. Find 31.

The lord's family emblem was displayed in many places. Try to find 10.

Stuffed swan was often served at feasts. Can you see the swan?

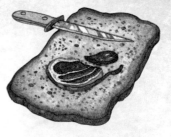

On the lower tables, people used slices of bread for plates. Spot 20.

The hall was lit by candles. Try to find nine.

Roasted boar's head was a popular dish. Can you see it?

Can you find 15 pies dropped by a clumsy page?

Tapestries hung on the walls. Spot five dogs in the tapestries.

Minstrels and entertainers performed during feasts. Find 12.

At a tournament

Tournaments were often held inside a castle's grounds. Daring knights charged at each other in mock battles, called jousts. Lords and ladies sat in decorated stands and many people joined in the fun.

A herald announced the names of the knights. Spot the herald.

Sometimes a knight wore a lady's token to show his love for her. Find two tokens.

A pie seller sold hot pies to the crowd. Can you see nine pies?

Knights jousted with long wooden poles called lances. Try to find 10.

Pages played at being knights. Find the page learning to joust.

The winning knight was given a cup. Can you spot the cup?

Can you see the page who has climbed up to get a better view?

Pickpockets roamed through the crowd. Can you see two?

Even priests came to watch the joust. Find two priests.

Knights wore splendid crests on their helmets. Spot four crests.

Wrestlers fought to see who was the strongest. Try to find four wrestlers.

Visiting knights had their own tents, called pavillions. Spot four pavillions.

Sometimes knights were wounded. Find a wounded knight.

Some people watched the joust from the castle. Spot three ladies at a balcony.

Squires helped their masters at the joust. Find seven more squires.

A family home

The lord of the castle and his family didn't live in their castle all the time, but they often stayed there. Here you can see the family in their living room, or 'solar', and in the castle grounds.

The lady of the castle planned feasts with the cook. Find the cook.

Puppets were popular toys. Try to spot seven.

Boys from noble families came to be squires at the castle. Find two squires training to be knights.

Babies had silver rattles. Spot the rattle.

Girls did fine needlework. Spot three pieces of needlework.

The family owned precious handmade books, called manuscripts. Find five.

The lord and his friends went out hunting. Spot six hunting horns.

The older children played chess. Find the chess piece their little sister has taken.

Children played with spinning tops. Try to spot four.

The castle was full of dogs. Find 14 dogs inside and out.

Many people had meetings with the lord. Spot the steward and the constable.

Herbs were grown to make medicines. Spot the lord's mother in her herb garden.

The ladies used falcons to hunt for small birds. Spot six falcons.

Some children rode hobby horses. Can you find six?

19

A crusader castle

Crusaders were Christian knights from Europe who fought to win land around Jerusalem.

This scene shows a king and his followers visiting a castle built by crusader knights.

This castle was run by crusader knights called Hospitallers. Find 33 Hospitaller knights.

Wild animals lurked in the hills. Can you spot six wolves and a lion?

Find a lady who has fainted from heat.

The castle baker ground his flour in a windmill. Spot the windmill.

Can you see the king who has come to stay in the castle?

The crusaders kept pigeons to eat. Find 29 pigeons.

Armed knights accompanied the king. Find nine mounted knights.

Some knights were attacked and wounded on the way. Spot the wounded knight.

Squires walked beside their masters. Can you see six squires?

Mules carried sacks of food supplies. Spot five mules.

Minstrels played to the knights and ladies. Find the minstrel.

The chief guard of the castle was called the castellan. Can you spot him?

Can you spot the bishop giving thanks for a safe journey?

An aqueduct carried water to the castle. Can you see the aqueduct?

A samurai fortress

Japanese war lords lived in well-defended fortresses with their fierce samurai warriors.

In peacetime, the samurai trained for battle and the fortresses were full of life.

The lord of the fortress was called the daimyo. Can you spot him?

Nursemaids cared for the lord's children. Find three nursemaids.

Samurai warriors marched around the courtyard. Spot ten small flags on the backs of the samurai.

Laundry maids washed huge loads of clothes. Find three laundry baskets.

Young samurai learned how to fight. Find eight samurai fighting with wooden swords.

Some Buddhist priests lived in the fortress. Can you see three priests?

Merchants bought silk to show the ladies. Find three merchants bringing silk.

The lord's children loved to fly kites. Can you see five kites?

Local farmers brought food to the fortress. Find four farmers with baskets of food.

Leatherworkers made saddles for the warriors. Spot seven saddles.

Sword-makers sharpened swords on stones. Find four sword-makers.

Tall banners were fixed to the fortress walls and carried by flag-bearers. Spot nine banners.

Samurai wore breastplates made from metal strips. Spot two metalworkers making breastplates.

Poets and musicians entertained the ladies. Find a poet and two musicians.

A Mogul fort

The Mogul emperors of India built vast, walled forts that contained beautiful palaces, gardens and mosques. This scene shows a Mogul emperor welcoming a procession of guests to his fort.

The emperor sat on a golden throne. Spot the emperor.

There were far more men than ladies at the court. Find 19 ladies in this scene.

Some palace guards were armed with muskets. Can you see four muskets?

Musicians played many different instruments. Spot four drums, nine curved and straight horns, and two pairs of cymbals.

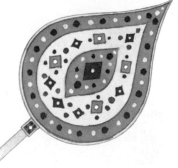

Servants waved large fans to keep the emperor cool. Find two fans.

Peacocks and monkeys roamed through the fort. Find ten peacocks and six monkeys.

Sometimes, poisonous snakes slipped into the courtyard. Spot nine snakes.

The palace artist painted pictures of important events. Spot the artist.

One mischievous monkey has stolen a turban ornament. Can you find it?

Can you see the prince who has come to visit the emperor?

The prince's courtiers carried ornaments on poles. Spot seven.

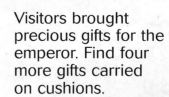

Visitors brought precious gifts for the emperor. Find four more gifts carried on cushions.

A romantic castle

Later castle-builders built 'fairy-tale' homes that looked like medieval castles but were much more comfortable. This picture shows inside a romantic castle, where a party is being held.

Huge banquets were prepared in the kitchen. Find the head cook.

Servants slept in small, plain rooms. Spot two servants' beds.

The castle had hot water for baths and flushing toilets. Find two toilets.

The castle roofs were topped by fancy weathervanes. Spot five more weathervanes.

Castle owners loved holding parties. Spot the king welcoming his guests.

Some guests waved to their friends arriving at the ball. Can you see 17 waving guests?

Castle-owners loved to live on mountain tops. Find three other castles perched on mountains.

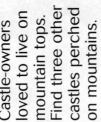

Musicians played romantic music. Can you see 13 musical instruments?

Some romantic castles had a 'grotto' that looked like a cave. Spot the poet in his grotto.

People could lounge on comfortable sofas. Find five sofas.

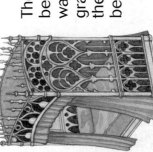

The royal bedroom was very grand. Spot the royal bed.

The castle had many dramatic carvings. Spot the stone dragon.

Oil paintings hung on the castle walls. Spot six oil paintings.

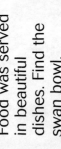

Food was served in beautiful dishes. Find the swan bowl.

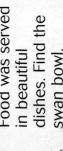

27

Puzzle answers

The keys on the next few pages show you exactly where to find all the people, animals and objects in the big scenes. You can use these keys to check your answers, or to help you if you have a problem finding anything.

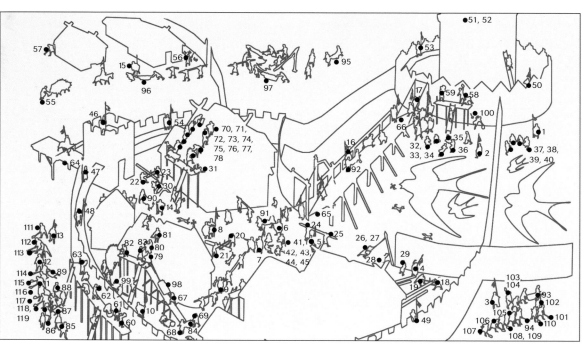

An early castle 6-7

Norman soldiers, 1, 2, 3, 4, 5, 6, 7, 8, 9, 10, 11, 12, 13, 14, 15, 16, 17
Carpenters sawing wood, 18, 19, 20, 21, 22, 23
Workers building palisade, 24, 25, 26, 27, 28, 29
Winch, 30
Falling Saxon, 31
Workers on lunch break, 32, 33, 34, 35, 36, 37, 38, 39, 40, 41, 42, 43, 44, 45
Lookouts, 46, 47, 48, 49, 50, 51, 52, 53, 54
Farm workers, 55, 56, 57
Builders applying limewash, 58, 59, 60, 61, 62, 63
Drawbridges, 64, 65, 66
Thatchers, 67, 68, 69, 70, 71, 72, 73, 74, 75, 76, 77, 78, 79, 80, 81, 82, 83
Stretchers, 84, 85, 86, 87, 88, 89, 90, 91, 92, 93, 94, 95
Sleds, 96, 97, 98
Hammers, 99, 100
Saxons with shovels, 101, 102, 103, 104, 105, 106, 107, 108, 109, 110, 111, 112, 113, 114, 115, 116, 117, 118, 119

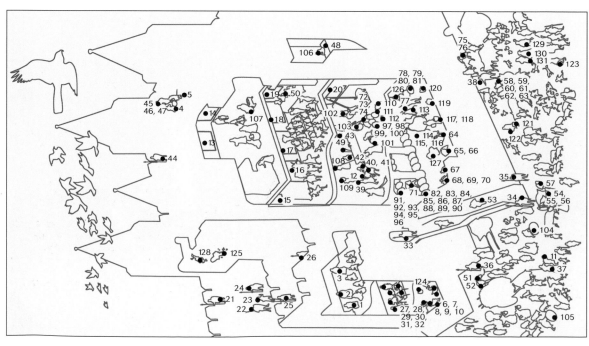

In the great tower 8-9

Priests, 1, 2, 3
Guards sharing snack, 4, 5
Prisoners, 6, 7, 8, 9, 10, 11, 12
Tapestries, 13, 14, 15, 16, 17, 18, 19, 20
Guards, 21, 22, 23, 24, 25, 26, 27, 28, 29, 30, 31, 32, 33, 34, 35, 36, 37, 38, 39, 40, 41, 42, 43, 44, 45, 46, 47, 48
Steward, 49
Lord, 50
Sacks, 51, 52, 53, 54, 55, 56, 57, 58, 59, 60, 61, 62, 63, 64, 65, 66, 67, 68, 69, 70, 71, 72, 73, 74, 75, 76, 77
Barrels, 78, 79, 80, 81, 82, 83, 84, 85, 86, 87, 88, 89, 90, 91, 92, 93, 94, 95, 96, 97, 98, 99, 100, 101, 102, 103, 104, 105
Guard on garderobe, 106
Lady working on tapestry, 107
Buckets, 108, 109, 110, 111, 112, 113, 114, 115, 116, 117, 118, 119, 120, 121, 122, 123, 124, 125, 126
Clerk, 127
Falling servant, 128
Merchants, 129, 130, 131

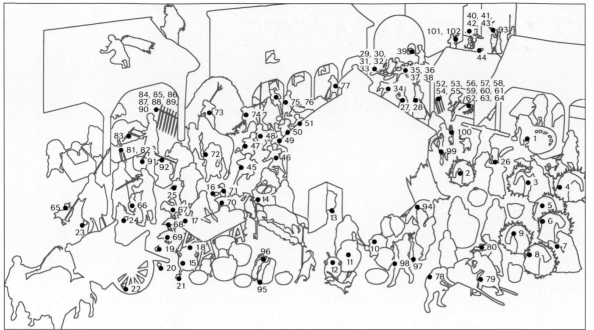

In the bailey 10-11

Carpenter making wheel, 1
Drying tunics, 2, 3, 4, 5, 6, 7, 8, 9
Cauldrons, 10, 11, 12, 13, 14, 15
Turnips, 16, 17, 18, 19, 20, 21, 22, 23, 24, 25
Milkmaids, 26, 27, 28
Loaves, 29, 30, 31, 32, 33, 34, 35, 36, 37, 38, 39, 40, 41, 42, 43, 44
Children playing ball, 45, 46, 47, 48, 49, 50, 51
Arrows, 52, 53, 54, 55, 56, 57, 58, 59, 60, 61, 62, 63, 64
Geese, 65, 66, 67, 68, 69, 70, 71
Farrier, 72
Stable boys, 73, 74, 75, 76, 77
Knife grinders, 78, 79, 80
Swords, 81, 82, 83, 84, 85, 86, 87, 88, 89, 90, 91, 92
Deer, 93, 94
Rabbits, 95, 96, 97, 98, 99, 100, 101, 102

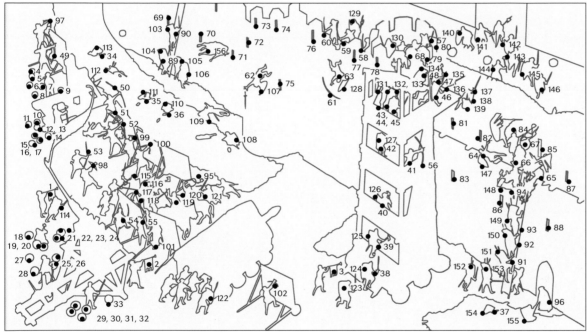

Under siege 12-13

Trumpeters, 1, 2, 3
Rocks, 4, 5, 6, 7, 8, 9, 10, 11, 12, 13, 14, 15, 16, 17, 18, 19, 20, 21, 22, 23, 24, 25, 26, 27, 28, 29, 30, 31, 32, 33
Swimmers, 34, 35, 36, 37
Men in siege tower, 38, 39, 40, 41, 42, 43, 44, 45, 46, 47, 48
Longbows, 49, 50, 51, 52, 53, 54, 55, 56, 57, 58, 59, 60, 61
Falling defenders, 62, 63, 64
Pots of fire, 65, 66, 67, 68
Arrow loops, 69, 70, 71, 72, 73, 74, 75, 76, 77, 78, 79, 80, 81, 82, 83, 84, 85, 86, 87, 88
Climbing or falling attackers, 89, 90, 91, 92, 93, 94
Morning star, 95
Spy, 96
Crossbows, 97, 98, 99 100, 101, 102
Shields, 103, 104, 105 106, 107, 108, 109, 110, 111, 112, 113, 114, 115, 116, 117, 118, 119, 120, 121, 122, 123, 124, 125, 126, 127, 128, 129, 130, 131, 132, 133, 134, 135, 136, 137, 138, 139, 140, 141, 142, 143, 144, 145, 146, 147, 148, 149, 150, 151, 152, 153, 154, 155
Flying cow, 156

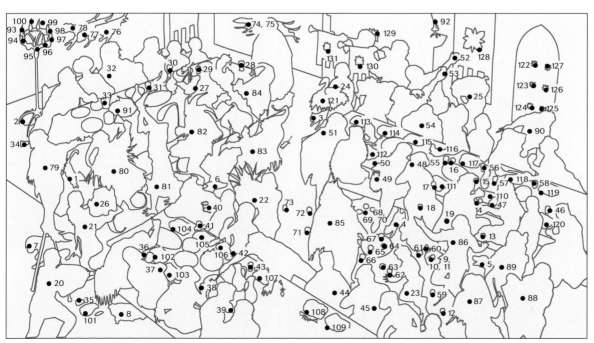

At a feast 14-15

Cats, 1, 2, 3, 4
Dogs, 5, 6, 7, 8
Juggling balls, 9, 10, 11, 12, 13, 14, 15, 16, 17, 18, 19
Servants, 20, 21, 22, 23, 24, 25
Marzipan castle, 26
Salt container, 27
Goblets, 28, 29, 30, 31, 32, 33, 34, 35, 36, 37, 38, 39, 40, 41, 42, 43, 44, 45, 46, 47, 48, 49, 50, 51, 52, 53, 54, 55, 56, 57, 58
Pies, 59, 60, 61, 62, 63, 64, 65, 66, 67, 68, 69, 70, 71, 72, 73
Dogs in tapestries, 74, 75, 76, 77, 78
Minstrels & entertainers, 79, 80, 81, 82, 83, 84, 85, 86, 87, 88, 89, 90
Boar's head, 91
Candles, 92, 93, 94, 95, 96, 97, 98, 99, 100
Bread slices, 101, 102, 103, 104, 105, 106, 107, 108, 109, 110, 111, 112, 113, 114, 115, 116, 117, 118, 119, 120
Stuffed swan, 121
Family emblems, 122, 123, 124, 125, 126, 127, 128, 129, 130, 131

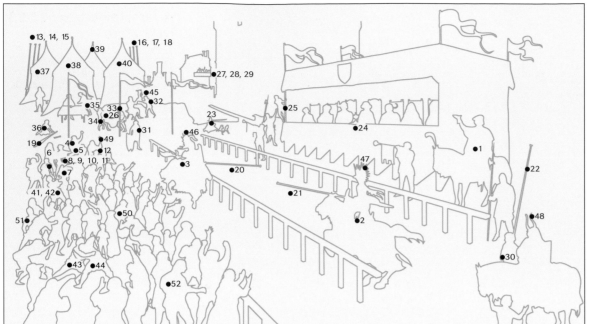

At a tournament 16-17

Herald, 1
Tokens, 2, 3,
Pies, 4, 5, 6, 7, 8, 9, 10, 11, 12
Lances, 13, 14, 15, 16, 17, 18, 19,
   20, 21, 22
Jousting page, 23
Cup, 24
Climbing page, 25
Wounded knight, 26
Ladies on balcony, 27, 28, 29
Squires, 30, 31, 32, 33, 34, 35, 36
Pavillions, 37, 38, 39, 40
Wrestlers, 41, 42, 43, 44
Crests, 45, 46, 47, 48
Priests, 49, 50
Pickpockets, 51, 52

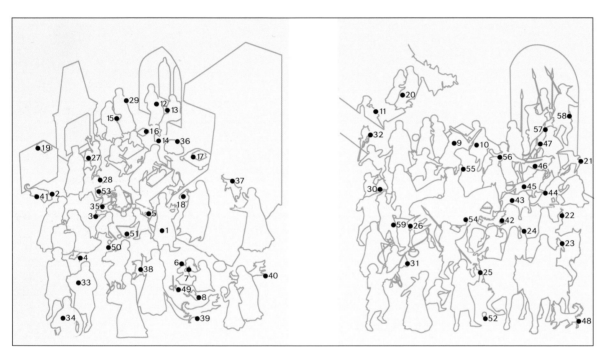

A family home 18-19

Cook, 1
Puppets, 2, 3, 4, 5, 6, 7, 8
Squires, 9, 10
Rattle, 11
Needlework, 12, 13, 14
Manuscripts, 15, 16, 17, 18, 19
Lord's mother, 20
Falcons, 21, 22, 23, 24, 25, 26
Hobby horses, 27, 28, 29, 30, 31, 32
Steward, 33
Constable, 34
Dogs, 35, 36, 37, 38, 39, 40, 41
   42, 43, 44, 45, 46, 47, 48
Spinning tops, 49, 50, 51, 52
Chess piece, 53
Hunting horns, 54, 55, 56, 57, 58, 59

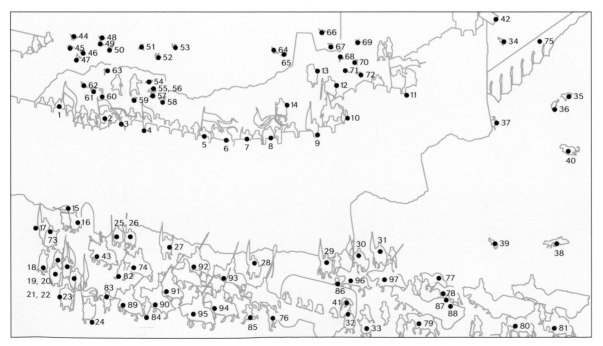

A crusader castle 20-21

Hospitaller knights, 1, 2, 3, 4, 5, 6, 7, 8, 9,
   10, 11, 12, 13, 14, 15, 16, 17, 18, 19, 20,
   21, 22, 23, 24, 25, 26, 27, 28, 29, 30,
   31, 32, 33
Wolves, 34, 35, 36, 37, 38, 39
Lion, 40
Fainting lady, 41
Windmill, 42
King, 43
Pigeons, 44, 45, 46, 47, 48, 49, 50, 51, 52,
   53, 54, 55, 56, 57, 58, 59, 60, 61, 62,
   63, 64, 65, 66, 67, 68, 69, 70, 71, 72
Castellan, 73
Bishop, 74
Aqueduct, 75
Minstrel, 76
Mules, 77, 78, 79, 80, 81
Squires, 82, 83, 84, 85, 86, 87
Wounded knight, 88
Mounted knights, 89, 90, 91, 92, 93, 94,
   95, 96, 97

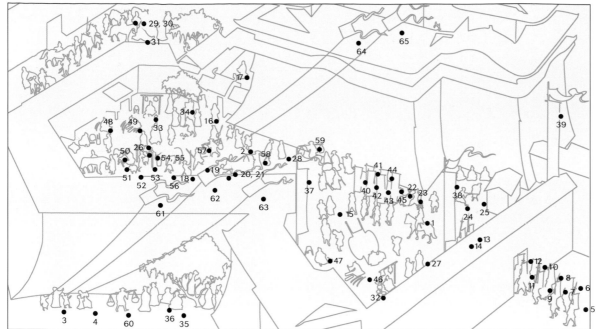

A samurai fortress 22-23

Daimyo, 1
Nursemaids, 2, 3, 4
Flags, 5, 6, 7, 8, 9, 10, 11, 12, 13, 14
Laundry baskets, 15, 16, 17
Samurai fighting with wooden swords, 18, 19, 20, 21, 22, 23, 24, 25
Priests, 26, 27, 28
Merchants, 29, 30, 31
Metalworkers, 32, 33
Poet, 34
Musicians, 35, 36
Banners, 37, 38, 39, 40, 41, 42, 43, 44, 45
Swordmakers, 46, 47, 48, 49
Saddles, 50, 51, 52, 53, 54, 55, 56
Farmers, 57, 58, 59, 60
Kites, 61, 62, 63, 64, 65

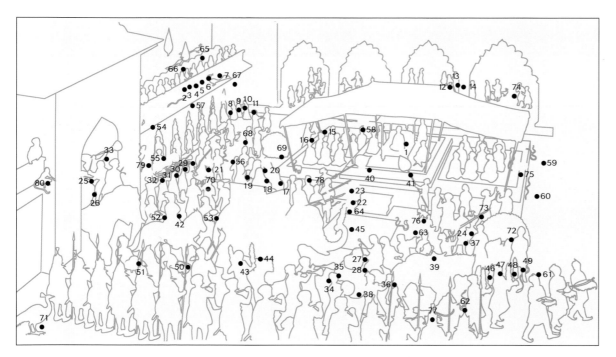

A Mogul fort 24-25

Emperor, 1,
Ladies, 2, 3, 4, 5, 6, 7, 8, 9, 10, 11, 12, 13, 14, 15, 16, 17, 18, 19, 20
Muskets, 21, 22, 23, 24
Drums, 25, 26, 27, 28
Horns, 29, 30, 31, 32, 33, 34, 35, 36, 37
Cymbals, 38, 39
Fans, 40, 41
Indian prince, 42
Ornaments on poles, 43, 44, 45, 46, 47, 48, 49
Gifts on cushions, 50, 51, 52, 53
Turban ornament, 54
Artist, 55
Snakes, 56, 57, 58, 59, 60, 61, 62, 63, 64
Peacocks, 65, 66, 67, 68, 69, 70, 71, 72, 73, 74
Monkeys, 75, 76, 77, 78, 79, 80

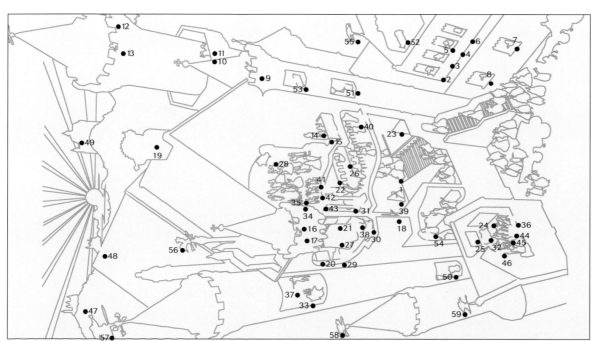

A romantic castle 26-27

King, 1
Waving guests, 2, 3, 4, 5, 6, 7, 8, 9, 10, 11, 12, 13, 14, 15, 16, 17, 18
Stone dragon, 19
Oil paintings, 20, 21, 22, 23, 24, 25
Swan bowl, 26
Royal bed, 27
Sofas, 28, 29, 30, 31, 32
Poet, 33
Cellos, 34, 35, 36
Flute, 37
Harps, 38, 39, 40
Violins, 41, 42, 43, 44, 45, 46
Castles, 47, 48, 49
Toilets, 50, 51
Servants' beds, 52, 53
Head cook, 54
Weathervanes, 55, 56, 57, 58, 59

Index

Photographic manipulation and DTP: Mike Olley
Additional illustration: Inklink Firenze

First published in 2004 by Usborne Publishing Limited,
Usborne House, 83-85 Saffron Hill, London EC1N 8RT, England. www.usborne.com